Color Your Way to a Life You Love™

GET OUT OF YOUR OWN WAY

A SELF-HELP ADULT COLORING BOOK FOR RELAXATION & PERSONAL GROWTH!

60 CALMING DESIGNS TO COLOR!
FLOWERS & NATURE
ANIMALS
MANDALAS
DOODLES & PATTERNS

ALPHA DOLL

COLOR YOUR WAY TO A LIFE YOU LOVE™: GET OUT OF YOUR OWN WAY

For information:
shellijohnson.com
alphadollmedia.com

Copyright Notice and Disclaimers

This book is Copyright © 2018 Shelli Johnson (the "Author"). All Rights Reserved. Published in the United States of America. The legal notices, disclosures, and disclaimers within this book are copyrighted by the Internet Attorneys Association LLC and licensed for use by the Author in this book. All rights reserved.

No part of this book may be reproduced or transmitted in any form or by any means, electronic or mechanical, including photocopying, recording, or by an information storage and retrieval system — except by a reviewer who may quote brief passages in a review to be printed in a magazine, newspaper, blog, or website — without permission in writing from the Author. For information, please contact the Author at the following website address: shellijohnson.com/contact

For more information, please read the "Disclosures and Disclaimers" section at the end of this book.

First Paperback Print Edition, March 2018

Published by Alpha Doll Media, LLC (the "Publisher").

ISBN: 978-0-9747109-7-6

WELCOME TO THE
COLOR YOUR WAY TO A LIFE YOU LOVE™
COLORING BOOK SERIES!

 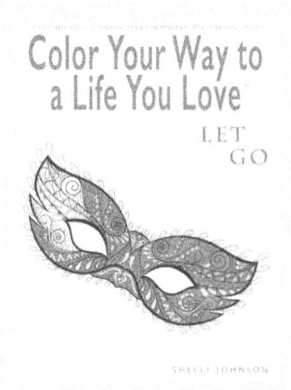 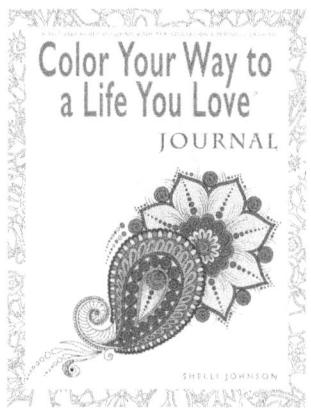

AVAILABLE NOW OR COMING SOON!

UNLEASH YOUR INNER CREATOR & MAKE IT YOUR OWN!

This is not just another coloring book, it's also an invitation for you to delve deeper into who you are so you can find out what makes you come alive. I'm a big believer in the power of taking small steps to get you anywhere you need or want to go. With that in mind, I invite you inside these pages on a creative self-help adventure. You'll unleash your artistic side with designs and patterns while you do daily small-sized activities aimed at: 1. helping you heal yourself and 2. inspiring you to create a life you love. My hope is that you'll use these pages to ignite your imagination, discard your limitations, and free your inner creator.

Feel free to add your own personal embellishments to any image. You can make each page as unique as you like by adding doodles, patterns, and/or shapes. Color the images any way you like with any tools you like. There are no rules except that you relax, enjoy, and color in a way that feels right to you.

THE MEANING & PURPOSE OF LIFE!

"The meaning of life is to find your gift. The purpose of life is to give it away."
—Pablo Picasso

THE PSYCHOLOGY OF COLOR!

From my layman's understanding of the meaning of colors, certain colors can evoke certain emotions.

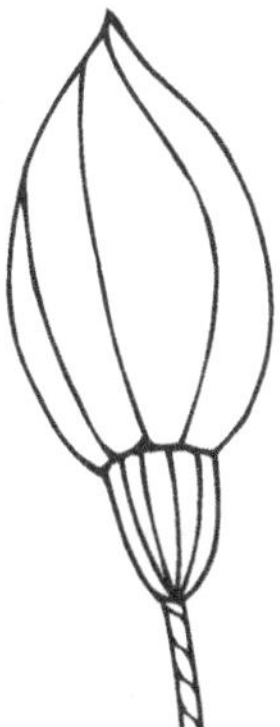

BLUE: centered, calm, hopeful, confidence
GREEN: growth, safety, endurance, calm
ORANGE: energy, happiness, encouragement, excitement
RED: passion, energy, strength, power, determination
YELLOW: joy, energy, cheerfulness
BROWN: stability
PURPLE: power, ambition, creativity, energy
BLACK: power, elegance, mystery
WHITE: light, goodness, safety

So keep that in mind as you color. If you're looking to experience a particular emotion/feeling/mood, you may want to use a particular color to help you get there.

A FEW HELPFUL SUGGESTIONS!

BABY STEPS
I'm a big believer in the power of taking baby steps to get you anywhere you need or want to go, which is why this coloring book is written the way it is. Each day has small-sized activities. They build on each other, one to the next. So feel free to color whichever image you'd like, just know you'll be best served to do the daily activities in order.

NO PERFECTION NEEDED
Do yourself a kindness and make a mistake in this coloring book early on. Scribble on some of the pages. Spill your favorite beverage on the cover. Rip one of the corners off. Color outside the lines. Make this book imperfect so that you'll feel free to be your real, honest self inside the pages. Being real, not being perfect, is what's going to heal you and set you free.

BE HONEST
I'd recommend that you don't show your answers inside this coloring book to anyone. Keep them to yourself for right now until you make it all the way through Day 30. Why? Honesty with yourself is what's going to help you heal and grow. You won't be completely honest if you're worried about someone reading your answers. In fact, what you're likely to do is tweak your responses, edit them, or scratch them out entirely if you're worried about how others might perceive you. So be kind to yourself & let this coloring book be just for you.

BE WILLING & OPEN
The first step to change is to be open & willing to it. You picked up this coloring book because you're struggling in this area of your life. If you want things to be different, well, both you & those things are going to have to change. So be open to experiencing something new & be willing to do the effort to get there.

GIVE YOURSELF PERMISSION
It's hugely important to give yourself permission (whether that's verbally or written) to: do the daily steps in this book, be/have/do/say/believe whatever you need to so that you can heal yourself, give yourself unlimited tries as many times as it takes, believe in your own worth and value, choose to create a life you love because you matter. Whenever you feel like you need someone else's permission to make a choice about your life, you just give that permission to yourself. The only permission you ever need to live your own life is your own.

YOU'RE ON A JOURNEY
It doesn't matter how old you are, how many times you've tried, or how far there is left to go. It's never too late to be the person you want to be. It's okay if you don't know things yet. You're on a journey and you'll figure it out as you go. This coloring book is designed to help you do just that.

BEGIN YOUR DAY WITH A STEP
If at all possible, do your daily step shortly after you wake up. That way, you'll be able to focus on yourself (because you're absolutely worth the time to do that) before your day gets away from you. So grab your favorite beverage. Find a quiet place. Relax and reflect while you're being creative.

IT'S A PRACTICE & A PROCESS
There's no doing this perfectly, and that's okay. You strive for progress. You do the best you can. So show yourself some patience and kindness because self-compassion is what you most need to heal yourself. You will make mistakes, there's just no way around it. Don't ever use any mistake as a reason to give up on yourself. Just circle back around and start again. And know this: every mistake is simply a brand new chance to do it better the next time.

AND FINALLY . . .
Remember (not just for this book but for all of life): you get out what you put in. So make yourself a priority in your own life because: 1. you're absolutely worth the effort and 2. no one else can do it for you. And one last suggestion good both for this book and for all of life: be brave and color outside the lines, that's where freedom lies.

THOSE WHO ARE BRAVE ARE FREE!

"It is not the critic who counts; not the man who points out how the strong man stumbles, or where the doer of deeds could have done them better. The credit belongs to the man who is actually in the arena, whose face is marred by dust and sweat and blood; who strives valiantly; who errs, who comes short again and again, because there is no effort without error and shortcoming; but who does actually strive to do the deeds; who knows great enthusiasms, the great devotions; who spends himself in a worthy cause; who at the best knows in the end the triumph of high achievement, and who at the worst, if he fails, at least fails while daring greatly, so that his place shall never be with those cold and timid souls who neither know victory nor defeat."

—Theodore Roosevelt

Source: excerpt (also known as *The Man In The Arena*) from the speech "Citizenship in a Republic" delivered at The Sorbonne in Paris, France on April 23, 1910.

COLOR TEST PAGE

COLOR TEST PAGE

Self-trust is the first secret of success.
—Ralph Waldo Emerson

1

1. Today, relax.
2. Take a deep breath in through your nose.
3. Hold it for three seconds.
4. Let it out through your mouth.
5. Then pull your shoulders down away from your ears.
6. Repeat five times.
7. Massage your temples & the back of your neck.
8. Repeat often, especially every time you feel like you're getting in your own way.

2

1. Today, know that you are not alone.
2. You may feel alone. You may feel like everyone else is happy, has their entire life in order, & is moving forward while you are stuck going around in circles.
3. But know this: 1. you're comparing yourself with others (which is a cruel act of self-abuse) & 2. you likely don't know just how long they were stuck in self-sabotage before they figured their way out.
4. So don't be so hard on yourself. Instead, remind yourself that you're not alone, that you are in fact in excellent company with the rest of us who are/ have been getting in our own way, as often as needed.

3

1. Today, befriend yourself.
2. Know this: you are with you 24/7. You are the closest & best friend you'll ever have. Getting in your own way by making choices that don't serve you is not being a friend to yourself; rather, it's an act of self-abuse.
3. So resolve today to have your own back *always*. Choose to make decisions & take actions that help you & not harm you, that are in your best interests, that aid you in getting to where you most want to be, just like a good friend would.
4. Now go do something nice for yourself.

4

1. Today, listen for your voice of wisdom (also known as your intuition).
2. Know this: your intuition is full of wisdom. It'll *never* tear you down or berate you or harm you. It'll *always* encourage you, strengthen you, & help you grow, even if what it's saying you need to do to move forward & out of the self-sabotage cycle scares you. Be alone for 15 minutes to listen for your intuition.
3. Ask questions about your life like: *Which actions do I do that sabotage me? Do I believe I'm brave/strong/worthy/smart/tenacious? Do I truly want to stop sabotaging my own efforts so I can move forward & create a life I love?* Write your answers.
4. Pick those thoughts that give you courage & read them aloud. Repeat often.

1. Today, trust yourself.
2. Read your answers from Day 4.
3. Now listen for your intuition as you write an answer to this: *Why do I believe that others know me & my wants/needs/talents/gifts/passions/goals better than I do?*
4. You have lived with yourself all these years, so trust, *just trust*, that you really do have all the answers you need to guide your life inside of you & you really do know what's best for you.

6

1. Today, trust your body.
2. Know this: it's likely that your body knows the choice(s) you need to make long before your mind does. Your body reacts immediately & makes an instant judgment. Your mind filters information through a lifetime of knowledge/feelings/thoughts then does pros & cons.
3. When making choices today & *every day*, pay close attention to how your body feels/reacts, *especially when you are getting in your own way* (which will make recognizing self-sabotage easier & easier for you).

7

1. Today, trust your intuition.
2. Know this: your intuition includes *both your mind & your body*.
3. Know this too: getting in your own way happens most often when you refuse to listen to & act upon your own intuition. But you have an intuition for a reason. It knows what you most want & also what you need to do to get it. Your intuition will guide you to a life you love if you'll just let it.
4. Write an answer to this: *What action(s) is my intuition telling me that I need to do to get out of self-sabotage & move forward from here?*
5. Then heed your intuition & do what it tells you to do even if that scares you.

8

1. Today, look at the big picture.
2. Write a list of moments (both big crossroad-type moments & itty-bitty moments) in your life where you regret the choice you made, especially if that choice took you further away from what you wanted.
3. For each one, write an answer to these: *Did I pause to listen for my intuition before making that choice? Did I do what my intuition said to do or did I ignore it? How did my body feel in those moments? Did I pay attention to what my body was telling me? Did I trust myself?*

Trust yourself. Do what your intuition tells you to do even if that scares you.

9

1. Today, find out why.
2. Read through your list from Day 8.
3. For each moment, listen for your intuition & write the first answer that pops into your head (so no overthinking or editing) to this: *Why did I sabotage myself in that moment?*
4. Hint: the answer likely has something to do with fear.

Trust yourself. Do what your intuition tells you to do even if that scares you.

10

1. Today, play.
2. Let loose for a little while. Take your mind off everything. Get out of your own head for a bit.
3. Go hang out with someone you like or your pet(s) or by yourself, whatever will make you happiest.
4. Do something you *really* want to do. Have fun!
5. Come back rejuvenated & refreshed.
6. Repeat often, especially when you find yourself getting in your own way.

Trust yourself. Do what your intuition tells you to do even if that scares you.

11

1. Today, address your fears.
2. Know this: fear is the number one reason that people fail to achieve their hopes, goals, & dreams. Simple, ordinary fear. So again, you're not alone; you are in fact in excellent company with the rest of us.
3. So read through your answers from Day 9.
4. Find the common thread in all your answers & write it down.
5. Take note: that thread is likely your biggest fear & the major reason that you keep getting in your own way.

Trust yourself. Do what your intuition tells you to do even if that scares you.

12

1. Today, be honest.
2. Write a list of other things you're doing that cause you to get in your own way even if you justify them &/or don't believe they are self-sabotage.
3. Know this: *anything* that keeps you constantly distracted &/or going around & around & around in circles/cycles in your life instead of moving forward in a straight trajectory toward what you most want is self-sabotage.
4. Your list may include things like: addiction, beating yourself up, not facing reality, creating drama, comparison with others, bad relationships, etcetera.

Trust yourself. Do what your intuition tells you to do even if that scares you.

13

1. Today, keep an open mind.
2. Write an answer to this: *What other thoughts/behaviors am I using to get in my own way?*
3. Consider the possibility that not taking excellent care of yourself & meeting your own needs is self-sabotage. So is self-pity &/or convincing yourself that you're weak or incapable. Be open to the possibility of self-sabotage with anything else you use as a distraction &/or an excuse as to why you can't.
4. Now write an answer to this: *How are those thoughts/behaviors serving me?*

Trust yourself. Do what your intuition tells you to do even if that scares you.

14

1. Today, find out what you believe.
2. Know this: you will live out what you believe. Your beliefs either make the walls of the box that confines you or your beliefs allow you to expand into the person you want to become. It's your choice.
3. So write answers to these: *Do I believe I am worthy of being the person I most want to be? Do I believe I am enough as-is? Do I believe I am deserving of good things/success/love/happiness/etcetera? Do I believe I matter (& therefore what I do matters)? Do I believe there is enough for me?*

Trust yourself. Do what your intuition tells you to do even if that scares you.

15

1. Today, figure out what you're waiting for.
2. Know this: all the time spent waiting is all the time you can never get back.
3. So write an answer to this: *Just what am I waiting to happen so I can move forward on a straight trajectory toward what I most want?*
4. Your answers might include things like: other people's approval/validation, the fear to ease, to feel qualified/experienced, to believe you're ready, to have more money/time/support/etcetera.

Trust yourself. Do what your intuition tells you to do even if that scares you.

16

1. Today, figure out why you're procrastinating.
2. Know this: getting in your own way is likely a procrastination tactic; as long as you're busy with activities/behaviors that keep you distracted &/or going in circles/cycles, you don't have to move forward in your life. Procrastination is fueled by fear. Read your answer from Day 11. That's likely your biggest fear.
3. Now write an answer to this: *What do I gain by delaying/postponing?*
4. Your answers might include things like: to stay in your comfort zone, to minimize risk, to keep everything the same, to reinforce your beliefs, etcetera.

Trust yourself. Do what your intuition tells you to do even if that scares you.

17

1. Today, realize what you're trying to control.
2. Know this: you're also likely getting in your own way because you cannot control the outcome & uncertainty is scary.
3. Know this too: absolute security is an illusion. There are no guarantees of either safety or comfort in nature. Avoiding fear of the outcome may make you *feel* safe but will not actually *keep* you safe. Fear is a legitimate excuse to not move forward *only* if the outcome could result in your maiming/death.
4. Write a list of outcomes you want & your fear(s) if you don't get them.

Trust yourself. Do what your intuition tells you to do even if that scares you.

18

1. Today, trust your instincts.
2. Know this: you *do* know your own wants/needs/goals better than anyone.
3. Know this too: on the other side of fear is where you will find freedom.
4. So read through your answers from Days 11-17. Write down the common thread in your answers. Then pause & listen for your intuition as you write an answer to this: *What steps do I need to take to move right through that fear?*
5. Take a deep breath. Then take the first step (tiny, if need be) through that fear. Repeat *daily*, one deep breath & one (tiny) step, over & over again.

Trust yourself. Do what your intuition tells you to do even if that scares you.

19

1. Today, realize the truth.
2. Know this: you're also likely sabotaging yourself by hiding your authentic self & by hiding your gifts/talents/passions because being vulnerable & letting people see the real you is scary.
3. Know this too: hiding your abilities serves no one, least of all yourself.
4. So write a list of things you are good at, things that you love to do, things that light a spark in you, things that make you feel the most alive.
5. Now circle the ones that you hide from the world.

Trust yourself. Heed your intuition. Breathe & move through the fear.

20

1. Today, keep an open mind again.
2. Consider the possibility that you are getting in your own way to keep yourself nonthreatening &/or less intimidating to others. Maybe so that they will be comfortable around you & so that you can belong & be liked & blend in. Maybe so they will stick around & you won't be alone. Maybe because they prefer you small & so you stay small.
3. But know this: you are sacrificing yourself at the altar of other people's wants/opinions; you will *never* find happiness & fulfillment that way.

Trust yourself. Heed your intuition. Breathe & move through the fear.

21

1. Today, understand your motivation.
2. Write an answer to this: *Just who am I living my own life for?*
3. And if the answer is anyone other than yourself, then write an answer to these: *Why am I choosing to live my life based on the wants/needs of others? What am I trying to gain by living for someone else? Is that making me happy?*
4. Your answers might include things like: you want people to like you, you're trying to prove your own worth, you don't want to take responsibility for your life, you want to be perceived a certain way, etcetera.

Trust yourself. Heed your intuition. Breathe & move through the fear.

22

1. Today, recognize the voices in your head that don't belong to you.
2. Know this: it's not others' voices that keep you in a cycle of self-sabotage, it's your own voice; you'll be victorious or defeated by what you tell yourself.
3. So write an answer to these: *What negative things (I can't do this/I shouldn't do that/I don't have what it takes/I'm not enough/I'm not ready/etcetera) are echoing around in my head? Whose voice(s) do those words actually belong to?*
4. Circle any words/phrases coming from a voice that isn't wholly yours (meaning it belongs to a parent/sibling/teacher/authority figure/etcetera).

Trust yourself. Heed your intuition. Breathe & move through the fear.

23

1. Today, speak strength to yourself.
2. Read your circled answers from Day 22.
3. Write an answer to these: *How is it serving me to allow these other people's voices in my head? What do I hope to gain?*
4. Choose (yes, it's a choice) to reject any voice that isn't wholly yours &/or isn't serving to strengthen you & help you grow. Now write an answer to this: *What supportive words do I most need to hear right now?*
5. Then read those supportive words aloud & reassure yourself. Repeat often.

Trust yourself. Heed your intuition. Breathe & move through the fear.

24

1. Today, believe there is only success or learning.
2. Know this: all the regret in the world won't change a single thing.
3. Now read your list from Day 8.
4. Write an answer to this: *What did I learn from each of those choices that I made?*
5. Let your answers strengthen you & fuel you to do better the next time, to move forward from here in a straight line with more wisdom & perspective.
6. Make this your mantra: *I believe there is only success or learning.*

Trust yourself. Heed your intuition. Breathe & move through the fear.

25

1. Today, be brave.
2. Know this: you & you alone are responsible for your own success & your own happiness. Remember that *every time* you make a choice.
3. So choose today & *every day* not to play into other people's beliefs about who you are &/or what you're capable of. Choose today & *every day* not to dim yourself & your abilities to the level of those people who would limit you.
4. Read through your list from Day 19.
5. Now be brave & shine one of the circled answers into the world today.

Trust yourself. Heed your intuition. Breathe & move through the fear.

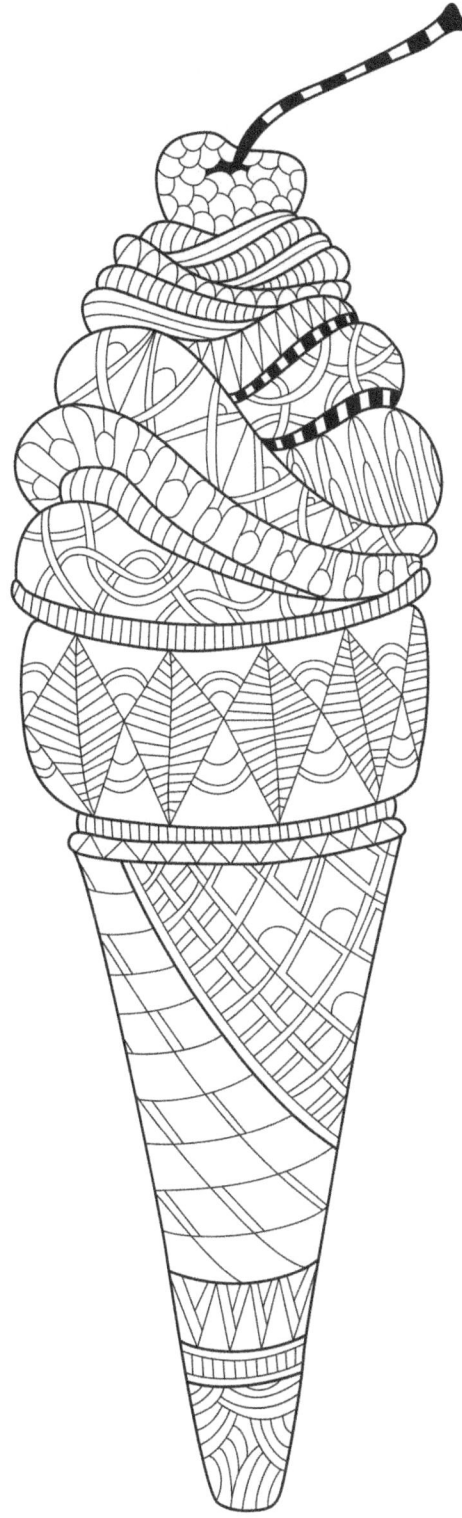

26

1. Today, hone your focus.
2. Know this: you also get in your own way when you start something new, then start something else new, then start something else new, & never finish anything. That keeps you busy, yes, but not productive.
3. So write a list of projects/ideas that you've started working on & then abandoned, except that they are still somewhere in your mind taking up your time & energy by thinking that someday you'll get back to them.
4. Cross off & let go of any project/idea that you don't have a passion to finish.

Trust yourself. Heed your intuition. Breathe & move through the fear.

27

1. Today, finish.
2. Take a look at your list from Day 26.
3. Pick *one* item from that list that is not crossed off. Choose the one you're most drawn to/passionate about completing.
4. Start working on it today.
5. Work (a little or a lot) on it *every day* until you finish it.
6. Know this: it does not matter *in the least* how slowly you go as long as you don't stop until you finish.

Trust yourself. Heed your intuition. Breathe & move through the fear.

28

1. Today, say *yes*.
2. Know this: if you want anything (big amazing things & small comforting things & everything in between) to happen in your life, you have to say *yes* first. If you say *no*, your journey down that particular path ends.
3. Know this too: you get in your own way when you say *no* to those people/places/things that interest you, matter deeply to you, &/or you feel drawn to.
4. So do yourself a kindness & stop sabotaging yourself by simply saying *yes* to all those people/places/things that will help you create a life you love.

Trust yourself. Heed your intuition. Breathe & move through the fear. Finish.

29

1. Today, relax into the journey.
2. Know this: adding pressure to yourself is also self-sabotage.
3. So do yourself a kindness & look at your life as a big experiment. Just see what works & what doesn't. Be kind to yourself as you learn & grow. Every mistake is simply a brand new chance to try again from a wiser perspective.
4. So breathe deeply, cut yourself some slack, let go of those things that no longer serve you, & simply take actions from now on that keep you moving forward in a straight line toward what you most want for your life.

Trust yourself. Heed your intuition. Breathe & move through the fear. Finish.

30

1. Today, celebrate!
2. Be proud of yourself for how far you've come.
3. Write down your successes & victories (big or small).
4. Do something nice for yourself (like a prize for a job well done).
5. Go & enjoy your life!

Trust yourself. Heed your intuition. Breathe & move through the fear. Finish.

ABOUT THE AUTHOR!

This book was born out of Shelli Johnson's own struggle with getting in her own way. She wanted and needed to heal herself. She wanted and needed practical and easy steps she could take to stop sabotaging herself so she could thrive. So she simply wrote the book she needed to read. Every day, she does her best to cut herself some slack & practice progress, not perfection.

Shelli's also an award-winning journalist (sports reporting), novelist (grand prize winner), and blogger (shellijohnson.com/blog). She's a truck owner, horse rider, photographer, yoga enthusiast, and slow-cooker fan (shellijohnson.com/recipes). Find out more at: shellijohnson.com/about

**Find out about Shelli's other books at:
shellijohnson.com/books**

GET YOUR FREE STUFF!

Visit: shellijohnson.com/signup
Opt-in for the newsletter to keep in touch.
Get a free bookmark to color.

ACKNOWLEDGMENTS!

My sincere thanks to people who make my days brighter:
Rollin Johnson
Heather Porazzo

Disclosures and Disclaimers

This book is published in print format. All trademarks and service marks are the properties of their respective owners. All references to these properties are made solely for editorial purposes. Except for marks actually owned by the Author or the Publisher, no commercial claims are made to their use, and neither the Author nor the Publisher is affiliated with such marks in any way.

Unless otherwise expressly noted, none of the individuals or business entities mentioned herein has endorsed the contents of this book.

Limits of Liability & Disclaimers of Warranties

Because this book is a general educational information product, it is not a substitute for professional advice on the topics discussed in it.

The materials in this book are provided "as is" and without warranties of any kind either express or implied. The Author and the Publisher disclaim all warranties, express or implied, including, but not limited to, implied warranties of merchantability and fitness for a particular purpose. The Author and the Publisher do not warrant that defects will be corrected. The Author does not warrant or make any representations regarding the use or the results of the use of the materials in this book in terms of their correctness, accuracy, reliability, or otherwise. Applicable law may not allow the exclusion of implied warranties, so the above exclusion may not apply to you.

Under no circumstances, including, but not limited to, negligence, shall the Author or the Publisher be liable for any special or consequential damages that result from the use of, or the inability to use this book, even if the Author, the Publisher, or an authorized representative has been advised of the possibility of such damages. Applicable law may not allow the limitation or exclusion of liability or incidental or consequential damages, so the above limitation or exclusion may not apply to you. In no event shall the Author or Publisher total liability to you for all damages, losses, and causes of action (whether in contract, tort, including but not limited to, negligence or otherwise) exceed the amount paid by you, if any, for this book.

You agree to hold the Author and the Publisher of this book, principals, agents, affiliates, and employees harmless from any and all liability for all claims for damages due to injuries, including attorney fees and costs, incurred by you or caused to third parties by you, arising out of the products, services, and activities discussed in this book, excepting only claims for gross negligence or intentional tort.

You agree that any and all claims for gross negligence or intentional tort shall be settled solely by confidential binding arbitration per the American Arbitration Association's commercial arbitration rules. Your claim cannot be aggregated with third party claims. All arbitration must occur in the municipality where the Author's principal place of business is located. Arbitration fees and costs shall be split equally, and you are solely responsible for your own lawyer fees.

Facts and information are believed to be accurate at the time they were placed in this book. All data provided in this book is to be used for information purposes only. The information contained within is not intended to provide specific legal, financial, tax, physical or mental health advice, or any other advice whatsoever, for any individual or company and should not be relied upon in that regard. The services described are only offered in jurisdictions where they may be legally offered. Information provided is not all-inclusive, and is limited to information that is made available and such information should not be relied upon as all-inclusive or accurate.

For more information about this policy, please contact the Author at the website address listed in the Copyright Notice at the front of this book.

IF YOU DO NOT AGREE WITH THESE TERMS AND EXPRESS CONDITIONS, DO NOT READ THIS BOOK. YOUR USE OF THIS BOOK, INCLUDING PRODUCTS, SERVICES, AND ANY PARTICIPATION IN ACTIVITIES MENTIONED IN THIS BOOK, MEAN THAT YOU ARE AGREEING TO BE LEGALLY BOUND BY THESE TERMS.

Affiliate Compensation & Material Connections Disclosure

This book may contain references to websites and information created and maintained by other individuals and organizations. The Author and the Publisher do not control or guarantee the accuracy, completeness, relevance, or timeliness of any information or privacy policies posted on these websites.

You should assume that all references to products and services in this book are made because material connections exist between the Author or Publisher and the providers of the mentioned products and services ("Provider"). You should also assume that all website links within this book are affiliate links for (a) the Author, (b) the Publisher, or (c) someone else who is an affiliate for the mentioned products and services (individually and collectively, the "Affiliate").

The Affiliate recommends products and services in this book based in part on a good faith belief that the purchase of such products or services will help readers in general.

The Affiliate has this good faith belief because (a) the Affiliate has tried the product or service mentioned prior to recommending it or (b) the Affiliate has researched the reputation of the Provider and has made the decision to recommend the Provider's products or services based on the Provider's history of providing these or other products or services.

The representations made by the Affiliate about products and services reflect the Affiliate's honest opinion based upon the facts known to the Affiliate at the time this book was published.

Because there is a material connection between the Affiliate and Providers of products or services mentioned in this book, you should always assume that the Affiliate may be biased because of the Affiliate's relationship with a Provider and/or because the Affiliate has received or will receive something of value from a Provider.

Perform your own due diligence before purchasing a product or service mentioned in this book.

The type of compensation received by the Affiliate may vary. In some instances, the Affiliate may receive complimentary products (such as a review copy), services, or money from a Provider prior to mentioning the Provider's products or services in this book.

In addition, the Affiliate may receive a monetary commission or non-monetary compensation when you take action by using a website link within in this book. This includes, but is not limited to, when you purchase a product or service from a Provider after going to a website link contained in this book.

Health Disclaimers

As an express condition to reading to this book, you understand and agree to the following terms.

This book is a general educational health-related information product. This book does not contain medical advice.

The book's content is not a substitute for direct, personal, professional medical care and diagnosis. None of the exercises or treatments (including products and services) mentioned in this book should be performed or otherwise used without prior approval from your physician or other qualified professional health care provider.

There may be risks associated with participating in activities or using products and services mentioned in this book for people in poor health or with pre-existing physical or mental health conditions.

Because these risks exist, you will not use such products or participate in such activities if you are in poor health or have a pre-existing mental or physical condition. If you choose to participate in these risks, you do so of your own free will and accord, knowingly and voluntarily assuming all risks associated with such activities.

Earnings & Income Disclaimers
No Earnings Projections, Promises or Representations

For purposes of these disclaimers, the term "Author" refers individually and collectively to the author of this book and to the affiliate (if any) whose affiliate hyperlinks are referenced in this book.

You recognize and agree that the Author and the Publisher have made no implications, warranties, promises, suggestions, projections, representations or guarantees whatsoever to you about future prospects or earnings, or that you will earn any money, with respect to your purchase of this book, and that the Author and the Publisher have not authorized any such projection, promise, or representation by others.

Any earnings or income statements, or any earnings or income examples, are only estimates of what you might earn. There is no assurance you will do as well as stated in any examples. If you rely upon any figures provided, you must accept the entire risk of not doing as well as the information provided. This applies whether the earnings or income examples are monetary in nature or pertain to advertising credits which may be earned (whether such credits are convertible to cash or not).

There is no assurance that any prior successes or past results as to earnings or income (whether monetary or advertising credits, whether convertible to cash or not) will apply, nor can any prior successes be used, as an indication of your future success or results from any of the information, content, or strategies. Any and all claims or representations as to income or earnings (whether monetary or advertising credits, whether convertible to cash or not) are not to be considered as "average earnings".

Testimonials & Examples

Testimonials and examples in this book are exceptional results, do not reflect the typical purchaser's experience, do not apply to the average person and are not intended to represent or guarantee that anyone will achieve the same or similar results. Where specific income or earnings (whether monetary or advertising credits, whether convertible to cash or not), figures are used and attributed to a specific individual or business, that individual or business has earned that amount. There is no assurance that you will do as well using the same information or strategies. If you rely on the specific income or earnings figures used, you must accept all the risk of not doing as well. The described experiences are atypical. Your financial results are likely to differ from those described in the testimonials.

The Economy

The economy, where you do business, on a national and even worldwide scale, creates additional uncertainty and economic risk. An economic recession or depression might negatively affect your results.

Your Success or Lack of It

Your success in using the information or strategies provided in this book depends on a variety of factors. The Author and the Publisher have no way of knowing how well you will do because they do not know you, your background, your work ethic, your dedication, your motivation, your desire, or your business skills or practices. Therefore, neither the Author nor the Publisher guarantees or implies that you will get rich, that you will do as well, or that you will have any earnings (whether monetary or advertising credits, whether convertible to cash or not), at all.

Businesses and earnings derived therefrom involve unknown risks and are not suitable for everyone. You may not rely on any information presented in this book or otherwise provided by the Author or the Publisher, unless you do so with the knowledge and understanding that you can experience significant losses (including, but not limited to, the loss of any monies paid to purchase this book and/or any monies spent setting up, operating, and/or marketing your business activities, and further, that you may have no earnings at all (whether monetary or advertising credits, whether convertible to cash or not).

Forward-Looking Statements

Materials in this book may contain information that includes or is based upon forward-looking statements within the meaning of the Securities Litigation Reform Act of 1995. Forward-looking statements give the Author's expectations or forecasts of future events. You can identify these statements by the fact that they do not relate strictly to historical or current facts. They use words such as "anticipate," "estimate," "expect," "project," "intend," "plan," "believe," and other words and terms of similar meaning in connection with a description of potential earnings or financial performance.

Any and all forward looking statements here or on any materials in this book are intended to express an opinion of earnings potential. Many factors will be important in determining your actual results and no guarantees are made that you will achieve results similar to the Author or anybody else. In fact, no guarantees are made that you will achieve any results from applying the Author's ideas, strategies, and tactics found in this book.

Purchase Price

Although the Publisher believes the price is fair for the value that you receive, you understand and agree that the purchase price for this book has been arbitrarily set by the Publisher or the vendor who sold you this book. This price bears no relationship to objective standards.

Due Diligence

You are advised to do your own due diligence when it comes to making any decisions. Use caution and seek the advice of qualified professionals before acting upon the contents of this book or any other information. You shall not consider any examples, documents, or other content in this book or otherwise provided by the Author or Publisher to be the equivalent of professional advice.

The Author and the Publisher assume no responsibility for any losses or damages resulting from your use of any link, information, or opportunity contained in this book or within any other information disclosed by the Author or the Publisher in any form whatsoever.

YOU SHOULD ALWAYS CONDUCT YOUR OWN INVESTIGATION (PERFORM DUE DILIGENCE)
BEFORE BUYING PRODUCTS OR SERVICES FROM ANYONE. THIS INCLUDES PRODUCTS AND SERVICES
SOLD VIA WEBSITE LINKS REFERENCED IN THIS BOOK.

www.ingramcontent.com/pod-product-compliance
Lightning Source LLC
Chambersburg PA
CBHW060515300426
44112CB00017B/2683